Life's Unknown Path

Frank D. Robinson

Table of Contents

To fade from love

To feel that need

For me to pray

I raise my hands

Her Love

To have your love

Writing with words

Waiting to feel love each day

Lord I look for you to stand by me

Untitled

Untitled

Asking for your

My

Blessed with love

Lord you are here for me to say

Looking long and far is love for me

Lord I look

Lost from words

Rejoice our lord

Untitled

You are my

I have this love I need you to see

Untitled

He, she

You are this heart with wings for me

You showed me ways I did not see

We walk through life, so much to see

Lord I believe

My heart is

To have true love

Life is special

Love is not

In the dark

Standing with you

Untitled

Untitled

I have my lord to comfort me

It is hard when a love one passes away

A fool in love, some may say to me

Lord I kneel

I am not

Untitled

I reach for

People will

Lord I ask

Untitled

Untitled

Untitled

Untitled

Untitled

You left to be with the lord this day

Untitled

Untitled

Inner peace

Untitled

I will not ask

If I

We lost someone special

Walk

Open

Joy to our lord

Have I lost?

Untitled

Untitled

Untitled

To dream a dream

Your love is

Look to me

This road is

I dare to say

Your love

Someone special

My heart is nervous

To hide

I walk with these

Chasing

To explain my love

Making love under a moon

Like a Rose

Like a rose, so beautiful and true

I think about that rose, this is you

With a rose, this vision comes through

Someone so beautiful, this is true

Like a rose, you're special in deed

Roses make me think of love I need

A rose to keep us together, to see

The most beautiful rose to receive

Like a rose, the one I love as mine

With a gift to make our love shine

To dream of you, this is no lie

My rose for me to keep love alive

Like an Angel

Like an angel, to be next to me

Down from heaven, to see my needs

With my heart to say "I love you"

Guide my way, to see me through

Like an angel, your love is true

A gift from heaven, with no clue

To make me complete, for love to be

I need your love to comfort me

Like an angel, the love I need

The answer to love you came for me

I ask for love to share my needs

To look for you to be with me

You Are

You are my sun, so much to me

My heart that is meant to be

Someone to breathe life into me

A chance for me to be complete

You are my love, a reason to share

This bond with my heart, I swear

To have you in my arms to see

My heart will know you are with me

You are in my heart, to receive

My sun, my moon, the love from me

If I am lost, I will not care

With you, I have nothing to fear

Lord I Come to You on this Day

Lord I come to you on this day

For wisdom, before I come to stay

Lord I come to leave words to say

Forgive me to kneel and pray

Lord I come to you on this day

I pray my faith will not stray

Lord I come to leave words to say

I pray for strength and love today

Lord I come to you on this day

Embrace this soul, to kneel, to pray

Lord I come to leave word to say

Asking for your love as I pray

My Soul

My soul is lost to make a stand

Waiting for my mate to understand

My soul is here for my special other

Will I find that true love, I wonder?

My soul is waiting for one that cares

Warm with love as her soul is near

My soul is lost, I'm afraid to say

To feel her love, my soul will stay

My soul will fade without a place

Not to be able to touch her face

My soul comes to life with her stay

Over time, souls find their way

I Lost my Love on this Day

I lost my love on this day

My heart lost a mate, to say

Memories of you, never to go away

To reunite with you again someday

I lost my love on this day

Waiting to hold you again, I pray

You give me completion in your way

To say you were my love that stayed

I lost my love on this day

Part of me never to be the same

You left this place, in God's embrace

Now my mate is in God's true grace

My Heart is Locked, Can you free

My heart is locked, can you free

My love bleeds for your desire to be

To find my soul, in pain for need

Desire for you is burning in me

My heart is locked, can you free

Your passion, my heart is dying to see

My soul will wait to feel your need

Your love lights this spark in me

My heart is locked, can you free

My desire and love for you to see

My heart will try to see your needs

Resting inside is passion to be free

Lord Who

Lord who is my father, I kneel to you

Your faith and love I know, is true

Asking for forgiveness, I pray for me

I kneel with no other place to be

Lord who is my savior, close to me

Bless this body, I pray for me

Embrace this soul, not to lose my way

Watch over my spirit to keep harm away

Lord who is my father, I kneel to you

Time and faith will see me thorough

I wake each day with life you gave

My heart is close to you each day

You enter this world, a day for me

Full of life, for the world to see

To watch you grow, for people to meet

A baby from heaven, God gave to me

To have you in my life, I need to say

God gave His miracle with love today

You are so special, I am complete

My life starts over with you and me

You enter this world, a day for me

Born from love, a miracle to see

To have you in my life, this I say

You came to mark this a special day

You enter the world, a day for me

I am happy to say, a miracle to be

Is this True, is this Meant to Be

Is this true, is this meant to be?

My heart needs you close to me

Will my soul lose the will to see?

Your love can show the way for me

My heart is looking out to see

Your arms, to show love for me

Is this true, is this meant to be?

Your love, finding my will for need

My heart goes on to speak for me

To offer what comes from love, to believe

Is this true, is this meant to be?

To show you are the one to receive

Lord I Pray, my Heart

Lord I pray, my heart needs to say

Protect my family, keep safe today

My faith with heaven will not stray

I know in heart, you are not far away

Lord I pray, my heart comes to be

With you, I kneel to heaven to see

I pray for your embrace to comfort me

To bless my soul as it walks with me

Lord I pray, my heart needs to say

You look in spirit when I pray

No one can take my faith away

Given to me by you, I know the way

You are Gone

You are gone, no words can really say

So many memories never die away

Your soul beats in my heart each day

The lives you touched are here today

You are gone, my heart hurts to see

Part is lost, why does it have to be

To lose your love, it is hard to go away

Never to be forgotten, my heart will say

You are gone, no words can really say

A blessing of love you were everyday

My soul is with you, never far away

You gave me love, no shame to say

You are gone, my heart hurts to see

No other has tamed my heart for need

So Many Things

So many things I need to see

For someone to share my life with me

Under the moon with someone to be

Hoping I am the one her heart needs

So many things I want to see

The one her heart turns for need

To be her love, no other for me

My love is all I hope she may see

So many things I look to see

To have her in my life, part of me

Leaving words to say can she believe

Trying so hard for this to be

To Be in Love

To be in love is something to see

Two souls look for a common need

My heart is lost for her to see

My soul needs to have her love for me

To be in love is something to believe

Our hearts together, I wish to see

My place in life, feeling love for me

Her desires are everything to receive

To be in love is something to see

My heart needs to know for me

Looking for love, I search for need

Believing in me is left for her to see

I lift this Hand to Touch your Face

I lift this hand to touch your face

Holding you with my deep embrace

To know your desire, I come to say

Dying to hold your love in ways

I lift this hand to touch your face

My soul kneels to be in place

I need your love to share with me

To show my love for your heart to see

I lift this hand to touch your face

Your love found my missing place

This love I own leaving with you

To show my desire only for you

Lord I Come to Kneel

Lord I come to kneel this day

Your faith is always special to say

I ask for your guidance, this I pray

Cleanse my soul to never stray

Lord I come to kneel and pray

To hold your love in my heart to stay

I know your spirit is here to stay

Strength and love is not far away

Lord I come to kneel and say

Thank you for being here each day

You give inspiration when I pray

As the Father, you show the way

To Have this Love

To have this love, I cannot see

Forever to roam, my soul will be

Unless her love can set me free

Feelings of desire cannot run through me

To have this love, I dreamed to be

I kneel before her to know my need

Is my time lost for her to see?

Faded inside if she is gone from me

To have this love, I cannot see

Praying she will hear love in need

Always lost, this soul lies in me

Only her soul can set me free

To Kneel and Pray

To kneel and pray to our lord today

I thank you for being here everyday

Believe in me, this I ask of you

Your teachings I know are very true

To kneel and pray you live today

Never shall my soul stray far away

On this day in words I say

Your love will save my soul to pray

To kneel and pray to my lord today

You gave me life to see home one day

You are my savior, I always need

To know in my heart, you believe in me

I Need your Love

I need your love, what can I say?

Hold this lost soul, let it stay

To wake with love I need each day

Reaching for your desire leaves to say

I need your love, how must it be

To give my love for you to see

Having your heart reach out for me

I pray my soul has yours to receive

I need your love, what can I say?

My love needs a place to stay

To join in hearts my love may see

I am ready if your heart calls for me

To Be Alone

To be alone, lost with words to say

Is she there for my heart to stay?

I pray she comes with love, someway

To sell my soul for her love someday

To be alone, my soul comes with me

Only her soul can move through me

Reaching for love so my heart can see

To understand what she may need

To be alone, my heart hides to say

Can she love me in time someday?

To give my love so she finds her way

Dying inside to show love this day

She is my

She is my moon, to give light to see

She is my sun, warming the love in me

Kneeling to show my love to see

This soul comes with much in need

She is my life, breathing in me

She is my soul mate to love and keep

My love to carry sinks deep to say

To know our souls connect and stay

She is my moon, to give light to see

She is my sun, warming the love in me

To live each day, she believes in me

My soul mate to love someone to keep

Kneel and Pray, My Heart will Say

Kneel and pray, my heart will say

To love and honor our Lord today

His words will keep from going astray

Willing to forgive, we come to pray

Kneel and pray, my heart will say

Believe in the Lord, this is the way

To have our Lord watching over me

You stand with faith, our Father, who believes

Kneel and pray, my heart will say

I live to believe your words today

Having your blessing when I pray

To know the meaning of your love each day

To Fade from Love

To fade from love, forgotten to see

My chest aches for love to receive

Resting for hope, love comes to me

With desire if I had love to see

To fade from love, my heart will say

Feeling pain until she finds my way

Needing love for my soul someday

Am I lost to always lose the way?

To fade from love, leaving the need

Without her my time fails to see

Finding her to make my life complete

Believing she is around, looking for me

To Feel that Need

To feel that need, I search to see

For this soul mate to believe in me

If my heart finds her love to be

Then this puzzle in life will be complete

To feel that need, time waited to see

A place with her only I can receive

Searching for love leaves me to say

In time, her love will lead the way

To feel that need, my time to see

Her desire can hold the love in me

Passion is locked for her love to free

Waiting to feel my heart can believe

For Me to Pray

For me to pray with a voice today

Never feel afraid to kneel and pray

To rejoice in His love, believing each day

We know our Lord is here today

For me to pray so you hear my need

To reach for heaven, our Lord will see

Closing these hands because I believe

You look to hear a prayer with me

For me to pray, our Father hears today

We honor you in life to know the way

Without questions, you are here to stay

I ask for forgiveness with each day, I pray

I Raise my Hands

I raise my hands to our Lord today

With faith, I live my life to pray

To die for our sins, you chose this way

We honor your name to kneel and pray

I raise my hands for you to believe

Your children are ready in time of need

Having your love, our Father, in deed

When time comes, heaven and I will meet

I raise my hands to our Lord today

To kneel and pray, I found my way

With this knowledge, I will not stray

To stand before you on my final day

Her Love

Her love opens my heart to see

I love her smile, close to me

To be her soul mate, I look to be

To fill her heart with love she needs

Her love gives my heart ways to see

To feel her kiss gives life back to me

In her arms, love has a place for me

I hope to show her the love I need

To ask her to believe what lies in me

I give my love for time to receive

To be together for her eyes to see

No one else waits to stand with me

To Have Your Love

To have your love, brings life to me

A place in time, my heart will need

With your hand, my heart stands to stay

A soul with soul, never to turn away

To have your love, I come to believe

Asking for your time to stay with me

Kneeling to say, "I love you" each day

With no other, I use these words to say

To have your love, brings life to me

As two hearts form to feel complete

Side by side, standing together to see

Having each other our hearts receive

Writing with Words

Writing with words, my heart will say

Opening my arms with love today

To desire this love you give to me

I love you more than words can speak

Writing with words, my soul will say

My arms are open to reach your way

Your desire, my heart waits to receive

Without you, our love can never be

Writing with words, my heart will say

Ready to show you love, with no delay

Remember these words I spoke from me

My life starts over if you stay to see

Waiting to Feel Love Each Day

Waiting to feel love each day

To walk this earth alone today

Left for me to wonder and be

Life is strange to wait and see

Waiting to feel love each day

Unless I have your love to stay

Leaving my time for you to receive

If you can open your way to see

Waiting to feel love each day

Now I wait to see if you will stay

I love you too much for me to stray

To hope your heart believes today

Lord I Look for You to Stand by Me

Lord I look for you to stand by me

My spirit believes the faith you see

You come to listen with those who need

We speak our faith for time to receive

Lord I look for you to stand by me

Made imperfect, I live this life to see

I kneel to talk, you never turn away

To listen and see what I have to say

Lord I look for you to stand by me

This spirit I carry will be yours to receive

My heart comes to you open, to say

I reach for your wisdom to see each day

Can you love this heart of mine?

To give my soul warmth to shine

To take this love I give from me

Not to second guess your love for me

I hope my desire is what you need

Only to give you all my love to see

Never to run, my love looks to stay

To enjoy your love with me each day

To kneel before you with desire to see

My love waits, should you ever need

To be in love, our heart could see

I only ask you to believe in me

Lord you made a place for me

You gave these eyes so I can see

A heart to feel your love in me

Things I am thankful to receive

With your love this comes to me

You are everywhere eyes can see

I know my Father, who created me

You are the reason I believe

When my times comes, this will be

Standing before my Father to see

Is heaven my home, a place to receive?

Family and friends to welcome me

Asking for Your

Asking for your time, will you stay?

For me to say, "I love you each day"

Next to you under the stars at night

The sky is beautiful with you in sight

Asking for your love, will you stay?

To try my best, never to be far away

Waiting to see, can you be with me

I open my life for you to receive

Asking for your love to find my way

Spending my life to love you each day

To walk with you, our hands held tight

A chance for you to see if this is right

My

My heart swam in pain, left for me

Until your love gave me a life to see

You saved my heart in time of need

To return the love you showed me

My soul was alone for me to stay

You released my soul, I am free to say

I need you to know the feeling in me

My love will always be yours to reach

My time was lost losing the way

Leaving me behind feeling alone each day

You took this life from terrible things

To show my heart there is a place for me

Blessed with Love

Blessed with love you gave to me

Left with love so hearts will see

Our souls as one to be complete

Not to look back asking, can this be

Blessed with love we now can see

To have our hearts come to believe

Trust with love we waited to see

We have one another to receive

Blessed with love you gave to me

Our hearts finally know where to be

To do the best our hearts will see

Love is always close to receive

Lord you are here for me to Say

Lord you are here for me to say

You gave me life to live my way

Watching over me with each day

My spirit grows strong, never to stray

Lord you are here for me to say

I kneel and pray, close each day

I live through life, from words to say

Knowing that you are a prayer away

Lord you are here for me to say

Kneeling before you, my Father, today

Praying for wisdom to guide my way

You know my faith, where this spirit stays

Looking Long and Far is Love for Me

Looking long and far is love for me

Where are the clues my heart will need?

Then there you were with beauty each day

My dream comes true if your love will stay

Looking long and far is love for me

Can we walk together for lives to meet?

To show you love my best each day

My arms stand empty to hold your stay

Looking long and far is love for me

Touch my hands they wait to receive

Your beauty and time is a world away

Hoping there is a spot for me to stay

Lord I Look

Lord I look for ways to see

Heaven lies above within our reach

You hear me pray as I give each day

You know it is not my way to stray

Lord I look to heaven, home to see

With no fear when times comes for me

To help those who ignore your ways

I pray they come to know your faith

Lord I look to heaven, waiting for me

Forgive my tongue because I believe

Your teachings are my path and way

You gave and give with faith each day

Lost from Words

Lost from words to find the need

To say what your love means to me

Is there answers showing my way

Feelings are telling me what I need to say

Lost from words my soul can see

There lies a spot for our souls to meet

Words are not easy for my heart to say

My love means more to show each day

Lost from words to explain for me

Why I fell in love with you to see

To handle your love with care each day

Because you are special in many ways

Rejoice our Lord

Rejoice our Lord, your voice to reach

Beyond the clouds, where heaven meets

Asking you to forgive our timely way

Knowing we live to pray each day

Rejoice our Lord, who lives to see

My spirit knows only one way for me

Believing in heaven to show our way

You look to us as we pray with faith

Rejoice our Lord, His time we need

Look no further for a way to receive

With wisdom, we walk your path to see

Doing our best to pray and believe

You are the air I need to breathe

This beautiful angel I truly see

To ask for another, I have need

Looking to you, the one for me

You warm my heart with your smile

Without you, love is an empty shell

Do I have to kneel for you to believe?

I will do so if your heart will see

You are my love to grow with me

Feeling your touch, the touch I need

The one I can see being my destiny

To live as one if you will walk with me

You are my

You are my vision, a dream each day

Someone I can hold to love away

Time will show our hearts, take lead

We wake each morning free to see

You are my life, this leaves me to say

Someone so beautiful to show my way

I was in need, my heart came to see

This search is over, a soul mate received

You are my love, I can hold each day

My heart fell in love without delay

For us to follow where loves takes lead

As with time we grow with ways to see

I have this Love I need You to See

I have this love I need you to see

Is it within your heart to retrieve?

Time will replace the words I say

With love I feel to show each day

I have this love I need you to see

To give only for your heart to receive

My life is open so your love can stay

Do you chance or turn this time away

I have this love I need you to see

To grow like flowers together with me

To demand your love I cannot say

It pains my heart if I spoke this way

You are my Father, here for me

Seeing your words placed to read

To look towards heaven close each day

I pray you will show me home one day

With this body, a spirit comes to retrieve

Your faith you gave to stay with me

Lord of lords, your kingdom lies in reach

I kneel to pray, my spirit will be free to see

You give me life with time to receive

Family and friends to know and meet

Time and faith to follow my soul each day

I pray with mercy, you forgive my ways

He, She

He who walks an empty heart to be

Has no love, if there is none to receive

She who walks feeling lonely to see

Looks for someone to share her needs

Meeting each other, they ask will this be

To give two souls their chance to receive

He looks to his heart to say, she is for me

To know with love, sharing her dreams

She looks to wonder, can he really be

To give her love a greater place to see

Standing together with hope to receive

Turning to each other to find their needs

You are this Heart with Wings for Me

You are this heart for wings for me

Someone from heaven, beautiful to be

These eyes can melt my heart away

To love you more the longer you stay

You are this heart with wings for me

To show my love so you feel complete

Are you going to lose those wings to stay?

My hearts waits to feel your love each day

You are this heart with wings for me

No one else can be this angel to see

If someone asked, did I find my way?

Yes, my angel made me complete today

You Showed Me ways I did not see

You showed me ways I did not see

Placing my love within your reach

Opening these eyes to beauty each day

To return this love, I pledge to stay

You showed me ways I did not see

These arms to have you close to me

Your lips that stole my breath away

To wake and feel your touch each day

You showed me ways I did not see

My soul has found a mate to breathe

To fill your life with my embrace each day

Deep within my chest, your love will stay

We Walk through Life, So Much to See

We walk through life, so much to see

Some for hope, others search for need

Few look in circles for what life will be

Many pass away before life was complete

.

We walk through life, so much to see

Some for happiness, others a place to be

Those who look with greed, lost to receive

Many fall in love, trying to fill their needs

We walk through life, so much to see

People look to find their hopes and dreams

Many wish the future will have lasting peace

So children can grow for their lives to see

Lord I Believe

Lord I believe, to reach and say

My faith is complete, always to stay

Asking for a blessing from heaven today

Looking at me to follow your ways

Lord I believe, to know your name

Showing you my best to live your way

Nothing will change my way in faith

I pray you will always keep my spirit safe

Lord I believe, to reach and say

Turning to you when I kneel to pray

You light my way, I know my stay

My time will come to walk home one day

My Heart Is

My heart is waiting for ways to say

Lost in time to reach love someway

This desire to find my place to stay

Leaving a world that is dark and gray

My heart is lonely for ways to see

Waiting for love to connect with me

Showing my arms to embrace your needs

A life together with hope and dreams

My heart is looking for words to say

To show my feelings so your love will stay

I kneel to speak, can you believe in me?

We can reach together for our hearts to see

To Have True Love

To have true love, allow love to lead

Bonds will show a path hearts will seek

Words are used, hoping love will stay

Take time to know where hearts will lay

To have true love, words lose their way

Finding something special for life each day

Standing together, two souls tied to stay

Giving love time to show hearts the way

To have true love, some push for need

Beyond their reach if used with greed

Many will say words are all they need

Standing as fools, blind to truly see

Life is Special

Life is special, god created His way

We see all around us everyday

Giving us places to pray our say

We look to our lord with ways to pray

Life is special, God created His way

Blessed heaven is close to reach and stay

Lord I come to speak in tongue to say

You created a world for us to pray

Life is special, God created His way

We live to know how your faith will stay

To believe my Father from day to day

Thank you Lord, who heard me pray

Love is Not

Love is not seen, if used for greed

We are blessed, but our hearts can see

Time will say where roads will meet

Greed walks alone in the dark to see

Love is not free, waiting to receive

Only to change, showing us destiny

What comes from the heart is left to see

Try to hide love will find this need

Love is not open for us to deceive

We hold no control over this destiny

To understand the life love will lead

In the end, two as mates to be complete

In the Dark

In the dark to feel my heart will stay

Alone with voice to speak and say

Will I escape, so my love can breathe?

For a chance to open this life and see

In the dark my soul was pulled away

Reaching to find the light of day

Then I heard this voice speak to me

Reaching out to guide my love to lead

In the dark I walked my past was seen

Now there is light, your love shines in me

Now I am free so our hearts can stay

To have this chance for love each day

Standing with You

Standing with you, my time to say

Offering this devotion from day to day

Sharing that part in your life with me

Opening my world to your hopes and dreams

Standing with you for love to say

You open my eyes to your beauty today

This world I see, that makes life complete

Only holds the love our hearts will seek

Standing with you for love to say

Our lives together to build a life to stay

Leaving one another with a path to see

Marked by love to follow and receive

Feeling your love going through me

Within this chest lies a heart complete

Life has changed with your love each day

Time will build a future for us to stay

You are so beautiful, I come to see

Leaving me with love, I truly believe

An angel who came to take the lead

Showing my soul the ways to receive

Feeling this way, leaving my life complete

Together our hearts have time to receive

You are everything I can feel in me

My love belongs to your heart to see

My hands hurt to touch your fire

The pain I except burns my desire

To lose my love, if your feelings expire

Your heart will come to know my desire

Waves will push to reach the shore

My heart keeps to the one I adore

You came and took my breath away

With love my life looks your way

My soul will die if I lost your desire

Gone with time to be without your fire

Leaving me to feel your warm embrace

You open my heart to a beautiful place

I Have My Lord to Comfort Me

I have my lord to comfort me

With His faith, my life is complete

Watching over me with love, I pray

To hear my voice to the words I say

I have my Lord to comfort me

My heart is not perfect, as you see

Forgive this spirit if I lost my way

Can you still love me, I came to pray

I have my Lord to comfort me

Embracing the time we come to meet

Heaven will lead my way to receive

The Lord and His angels, my eyes to see

It Is Hard When a Love One Passes Away

It is hard when a love one passes away

Do not cry or fear, God would say

His angels will guide you home today

To say the ones we lost are not far away

It is hard when a love one passes away

Our lord says, we will reunite one day

Things will be ok when we kneel to pray

To the ones we lost in heaven this day

It is hard when a love one passes away

They look from heaven, not far away

Time moves on but their love will stay

They are never far from our hearts each day

A Fool in Love, Some May Say to Me

A fool in love, some may say to me

I have the one to make my life complete

People can say I should stay away

My heart is deaf to the words they say

A fool in love, some may say to me

Your love will show where my life can be

Passing of time allows my heart to stay

Our lives will show they are wrong to say

A fool in love, some may say to me

People are lost to the love I received

We turn our hearts to the love each day

That escapes their minds, to know our ways

Lord I Kneel

Lord I kneel to speak my peace

Books with faith, I come to read

Your words I receive from day to day

Life has changed with these hands, to pray

Lord I kneel to show a way for me

Your love will find my path to receive

I pray to ask, can you forgive my ways?

Lord of lords to hear me pray each day

Lord I kneel for my faith to reach

The doors to heaven, when you call for me

Our Lord has ways He can hear us pray

Trust your faith to our Father each day

I Am Not

I am not rich, my pockets are not deep

No money to show you the world to see

I can't buy you fancy things to keep

To offer love instead of money or greed

I am not famous to give things for need

To know I am not these things to see

To be afraid, it might turn me to greed

To have your love means more to me

I am not special, others have more to see

To offer my love if you wait to see

Except me for who I am to be with me

I need you to see my love, to be complete

My waters of sorrow came before

With pain not having love to adore

Time was horrible to live this way

To see a world so dark and gray

It was you that pushed this pain away

To guide me so my heart can love today

Being alone was taking life from me

Stealing the love my heart needs to see

You kissed my lips for life to breathe

My heart is free to hold you close to me

My time was lost to show each day

I found your love in this heart to stay

I Reach For

I reach for your arms to comfort me

If you are sick, I come to your need

To feel your love waiting to receive

I ask that you give us the time to see

I reach for your hand, will you stay

The time to find love can start today

You can keep my love or push away

Or make room in your life to stay

I reach for your arms to comfort me

Leaving my hands in your life with need

Doing my best only your love can see

Asking you if your soul can join with me

People Will

People will say you are not cute

Some are blind to beauty, this is true

They have no clue what lies in you

A woman with love, if they only knew

People will look with things to say

My heart knows who I love each day

They do not see the love that stays

My love for you ignores words they say

People will question things we do

Strength and love will see us through

Our love is special, they will never see

We stay together because love believes

Lord I Ask

Lord I ask for I am a son in need

Kneeling in hope, love comes for me

Have I lost my way for something to be?

Unless my heart was blind and weak

Lord I ask how to find love someway

This heart is looking for a place to stay

Waiting to find where my love will lay

To share what lives in my heart to say

Lord I ask for I am a son in need

Looking for this soul mate to be with me

Time will say if she lives in reach

To show my love life can be complete

To walk through fire for you to stay

To feel the burn for your love each day

I leave my soul so yours can reach

To move with me finding lives complete

You are of beauty leaving words to say

To love you as our hearts grow each day

Feeling your touch takes my breath away

Replaced with a kiss from your lips to stay

My love will grow in strength with you

To start out slow to see me through

We have no clue where love will lead

This falls in place as time grows to see

To carry your love I have with me

When you are not in my arms to see

God did something special, this is you

My heart will not deny what is true

Part of someone special, I truly see

With your love, my life is now complete

You have no wings, my eyes can see

Looking so beautiful as an angel to me

Our love can grow with much to see

To find our way for true love to be

Hopes and dreams to know our needs

To move on with life together to see

Believe the words our Father can teach

We bow our heads for faith to reach

We trust our belief in the lord each day

Pray with your voice, I will not stray

Heaven is home, where our spirits will meet

Finding our family who will come to greet

Kneel and pray to be blessed each day

Listen to the words our lord will say

Do not waiver it is our lord who sees

His love is absolute for us to receive

Take the time to cross your hands and pray

Look to our lord and rejoice His name

My love escaped, leaving me no clue

Only to change when I found you

I lost my way for this heart to believe

Then you came to share life with me

The past was dark without hope for me

With you bring light for love to see

To know far and near this love each day

Your touch and kiss can lead the way

Feeling alone is gone to pass from me

I know how beautiful your love can be

Look to me so I may comfort your needs

Opening our book to write and see

Lord of lords, I will pray the truth

Kneeling with faith to believe in you

Some will deny where there spirits lay

I pray for those who turn faith away

Many are lost, leaving time to stray

Turning to those who refuse your way

Words will say, telling the way we pray

Listen to our lord who guides the way

Few will push for our hearts to stray

Look to our lord, the one who stays

Listen with faith, kneel and pray

For God to bless our spirits each day

You Left to be with the Lord This Day

You left to be with the lord this day

Hearts feel pain, your love will stay

You leave behind your memories today

People will question, why this way

You left to be with the lord this day

It came so fast without words to say

You leave with angels, who lead the way

God is waiting for you to be home today

You left to be with the lord this day

Love you showed lives with us to stay

We stand as one to leave words to say

God called someone special home today

To capture love, you will not see

It lies within us, waiting to receive

Listen with words should you need

Look how love has no face to see

Love will answer the calls for need

Looking for those who come to believe

In time two hearts bind as one to see

Finding their meaning for love to be

Love stays quiet without lips to speak

Keeping this special until time receives

Look with heart and leave your greed

Stand together to find that life you see

I find your eyes so beautiful to see

Your passion for love to comfort me

I see what was missing from life each day

Your love to travel in my body to stay

Can you look to these arms that reach

Walking together for our souls to keep

Heart for heart to equal love each day

I offer my time to complete your stay

Can you look to me if you are in need?

Always ready to keep your love in me

When I sleep, your vision comes to me

I ask you to be my hopes and dreams

Inner Peace

All I need is some sun and trees

Laying in the field feeling the breeze

Listening to nature to hear it sing

Nothing to worry about, not a thing

A beautiful place so hard to believe

My vision today I can see inner peace

All I need is some sun and trees

Laying in the field with you and me

Listening to nature to hear it sing

Nothing to worry about, not a thing

You entered a place to be with me

Sharing my vision for our inner peace

Call me a fool, this might be true

Say I am lost with nothing to do

Speak what come to guide your way

Or turn and walk with nothing to say

Call me the names that come to stay

See me a loser in your eyes each day

Laugh at me because of my beliefs

Say I am different in ways you see

I come to ask for your time with me

There is love inside my heart to receive

Give me a chance, there is love to see

Or walk away with nothing to believe

I Will Not Ask

I will not ask if you care for me

My heart will decide this path to see

Walk with me so you hear me say

Hold my hand if you chose to stay

I will not ask if you believe in me

This path you choose our lives will see

My time is here if you decide to stay

To extend my love with passing days

I will not ask you to be with me

My heart will wait for yours to speak

Your heart will know what to say

Take my love I give to you each day

If I

If I drop a tear, would you care?

Saying, "I love you" with words to share

Leaving your name in my heart to stay

Only to pass should you turn away

If I open my hands, would you receive?

My embrace, I offer in your time of need

My love is here with no reason to delay

So this heart can speak to you in ways

If I held your love so close to me

Can you give and show the same to me?

I kneel and say be my love each day

Will you except or look to turn away

We Lost Someone Special

We lost someone special on this day

Someone we love, words cannot say

God opened his arms to show your stay

To shelter his child with love, we pray

We lost someone special who flew away

To become God's angel, with peace today

Surrounded with love, in heaven this day

Opening the gates for you to live and stay

We lost someone special on this day

Wings will guide you to our Father today

Your spirit will live to look down our way

Memories of you will keep us in touch each day

Walk

Walk those steps in life next to me

Open the door allow your heart to see

Spend your days in my arms to stay

Except this hand for our love to expand

Walk and hear what comes from me

To tell you what is my hopes and dreams

I seen my path that was dark and gray

Take my love, only you can light my way

Walk with me for my life to be complete

Only your heart will know if this is to be

Time waits for no one to see this day

Our hearts will join, should they stay

Open

Open these hands, what do you see?

I see myself with you close to me

My life is so clear, you hold my needs

To feel and know your love through me

Open these arms for something to see

I extend my love with arms to reach

Hearts can dance to find and meet

Surrounding each other to be complete

Open my love that is locked from me

To answer the calls your heart may need

Leaving no questions, but time to see

You become my vision, to feel complete

Joy to Our Lord

Joy to our lord, His love we need

Someone special, we come to believe

Our Father in heaven, we know today

Listens no matter how much we pray

Joy to our lord, His faith we receive

Speak with His words, always believe

The blessings He gives find their way

Placing His love in our hearts each day

Joy to our lord, His love we need

Reach and pray your words to speak

Ask for nothing if you lie in greed

Our lord will know and always see

Have I Lost

Have I lost the will for love each day?

As if everything is falling far away

Where do I turn to escape and see?

Someone reaching for my love to free

Have I lost my heart to a place so gray?

Leaving me behind to walk and stay

Waiting for a light for reason to believe

There is someone that holds love for me

Have I lost myself to be pulled away?

To search for love in a world so gray

As with time if two hearts are there to be

They will come together to share one to see

There is this passion growing in me

I burn with desire to set it free

To open my heart for love to stay

Not to forget how it feels each day

To have the pleasure, I wait to see

For your love, I hope my life will meet

Can you see my love for time to stay?

No one really knows where love will lay

Fate came to me leaving eyes to see

Someone with beauty for love to receive

I look to join with you in life each day

To build a bond for our place to stay

With words my heart looks to speak

Feeling your love my heart will need

This soul is waiting for yours to stay

Feeling alive when I see the day

My heart lives with time to see

Storming inside this love to reach

Sharing your love to count the ways

Having with me, your life to stay

I spoke my words for you to receive

Is there a chance you will stay with me?

Giving my soul to yours each day

To start out fresh with love to stay

There is this path our hearts will seek

Finding someone our love can reach

Leaving us to guess where love will be

There are no maps that show our needs

Finding that life to know the way

Open your heart for her love to stay

Hearts can grow to find their roots

Showing this strength, for the truth

Walk with her to explain your way

Hide no feelings your heart will say

Remember each day if you find and see

Someone who will share love to receive

To Dream a Dream

To dream a dream I stand to see

Your lips are soft like a summer breeze

Leading the way for my heart to say

I never knew love like yours today

To dream a dream my eyes can see

Your time and love my heart will need

Leaving my life in your way to say

I will never allow my heart to stray

To dream a dream with time to see

In my dreams, your vision comes to me

Leaving your love in my mind to stay

Even in sleep, you are never far away

Your Love Is

Your love is my life, I truly see

Passion for love you give to me

You grow in my heart on and on

When you are far days are long

Your love is special in ways to say

To see us grow with passing days

My life does not see a place to be

Should you turn your heart from me?

Your love is a gift to have each day

Left with nothing if you turn away

Words are words these lips will speak

But your love will always grow in me

Look to Me

Look to me with an open heart

So we can talk to make our start

Do feelings of hurt block your way?

Keeping you from love to stay

Look to me leaving our chance to see

If we can fall in love for common need

Having this time in our lives to say

Our hearts will know to see the way

Look to me should you decide to see

What lies in my life for you to receive?

Will we share reasons for love to stay?

For you to know my heart another way

This Road Is

This road is here to take the lead

Will you walk this road with me?

To speak what lies in sight to say

My heart is here for yours today

This road is clear, I see in dreams

To reach your hand to share with me

To kneel and say with time one day

I offer this ring for you to stay

This road is here to walk with feet

Step by step giving love time to meet

You heard what comes from heart today

Will you build a life with me to stay?

I Dare to Say

I dare to say, are you real to me

Someone who has such beauty to see

Words are words that help me say

To know you more in time each day

I dare to say how you look to me

This vision of beauty comes to see

My way is clear for this heart to say

To take the chance for you to stay

I dare to say, spend time with me

To see how far my heart can reach

Our lives can live together to stay

I said too much from this heart today

Your love

Your voice is soft, light as air

I see beauty beyond compare

Standing between love and me

A place I hope you come to see

Holding you close to feel my kiss

Without your touch, lips will miss

Eyes so beautiful beyond compare

Days and nights for you to share

Time will move beyond our reach

Love can grow to feel complete

This road in life I walk is gray

Your love is my light turn this away

Someone Special

You are my life, you are my song

In my mind when days are long

Your beauty leaves words to say

Someone special in my life today

Sharing in love with passing days

Heart for heart the key to stay

Know the words you come to read

Pulled from my heart for you to keep

My life with you, my love to reach

There is no other to fill my needs

These words will leave much to say

Replaced by love to know each day

My Heart is Nervous

My heart is nervous when you speak

Your beauty is more than I can see

To surrender what is my heart today

Holding you close in life to stay

My heart is nervous with the truth

Sleeping at night to dream of you

Afraid to speak what I see each day

Your beauty is more than I could say

My heart is nervous to wait and see

The center of your love close to me

Day to day give me that chance to say

To honor and love you with each day

To Hide

To hide your heart until the day

You know inside one will stay

We are blind to know this fate

Love will come to have a place

To hide your heart until you say

Someone came with time to stay

One with one can you wait to see

Two hearts together love to keep

To hide what you keep from sight

Until such time things are right

People are left with different roads

Two will meet if love will show

I Walk with These

I walk with these two bare feet

Finding a place to pray for me

To heaven I look with voice to say

I live in life until I am home to stay

I walk with these two hands to see

Placing them together close to me

Lord you know when I come to pray

I never forgot who you are each day

I walk with these two eyes to see

My faith in god to always believe

Time will come when I am called away

To see my family and friends to stay

Chasing

Chasing to catch your love for me

If you give my heart time to reach

To know your way I need to say

I leave you room in my heart to stay

Chasing the beauty I see in you

Take the chance to know the truth

To listen and hear the words I say

Decide the path for your heart today

Chasing the desire my love will need

Will you take the steps to be with me?

My life was strange to leave no clues

To see myself falling in love with you

To Explain My Love

To explain my love there is no need

To walk in life for my heart to see

Looking for trust, to have both ways

To share in time, from day to day

To explain my love in ways to speak

Words do not play the part for need

My feelings will join this heart to say

Your love is missing from my life today

To explain my love, this will not be

If you can trust in us there is no need

I stood in time to wait and say

Steal this heart with your love today

Making Love Under a Moon

Making love under a moon, light fire

Your touch is fuel for this desire

The moon gives way for light to stay

Showing the passion from night to day

Making love under a moon for need

Hearts escape their bodies to see

Our souls have come to see this day

Pulled together with will to stay

Making love under a moon lit night

My love will always hold yours tight

The sun will rise for another day

Bonds of love are now ours to make

www.ingramcontent.com/pod-product-compliance
Lightning Source LLC
Chambersburg PA
CBHW070526030426
42337CB00016B/2130